Conversations with my Daughter on the Other Side

Conversations with my Daughter on the Other Side

The First Year

Barbara B Lauman

BALBOA.
PRESS
A DIVISION OF HAY HOUSE

ISBN: 978-1-4525-4856-2 (sc)
ISBN: 978-1-4525-4858-6 (hc)
ISBN: 978-1-4525-4857-9 (e)

Library of Congress Control Number: 2012904232
Balboa Press books may be ordered through booksellers or by contacting:

Balboa Press
A Division of Hay House
1663 Liberty Drive
Bloomington, IN 47403
www.balboapress.com
1-(877) 407-4847

Because of the dynamic nature of the Internet, any web addresses or links contained in this book may have changed since publication and may no longer be valid. The views expressed in this work are solely those of the author and do not necessarily reflect the views of the publisher, and the publisher hereby disclaims any responsibility for them.

The author of this book does not dispense medical advice or prescribe the use of any technique as a form of treatment for physical, emotional, or medical problems without the advice of a physician, either directly or indirectly. The intent of the author is only to offer information of a general nature to help you in your quest for emotional and spiritual well-being. In the event you use any of the information in this book for yourself, which is your constitutional right, the author and the publisher assume no responsibility for your actions.

Any people depicted in stock imagery provided by Thinkstock are models, and such images are being used for illustrative purposes only.
Certain stock imagery © Thinkstock.

Printed in the United States of America

Balboa Press rev. date: 3/16/2012

For and through Courtney

February 18, 1970–December 6, 2010

Preface

My daughter, Courtney, has helped more people since she passed over than she ever did when she was alive on earth. She wanted to help people while she was here, but got sidetracked by a 20 year heroin addiction. She would have liked to have been a drug counselor to help young people struggling with addiction, but she could never stop using herself.

She died on December 6, 2010 of an infection stemming from broken needles found in her thigh. The infection spread to her lungs and brain. She had over 40 abscesses in her brain. She was 40 years old. She lived the life of a cat with many lives. She survived too many overdoses to count. She survived homelessness, jail, prison, danger, a near amputation, (due to another infection caused again by needles broken off in her leg), seizures, a couple of strokes and rehabs that never worked for her.

At the age of 16, a gynecologist told her she would probably never have children. At the age of 28, she gave birth to my premature grandson, Gabriel Bleu, who spent his first three months in the NICU and had three intestinal operations in that time. She could have been a great mom, and was, mostly, for nearly a year, but heroin kept calling to her and by then, she didn't know any other way to live. At the age of 53, I became a full-time mother again.

Automatic Writing–Staying in Touch

The first time I tried automatic writing was about 30 years ago. The reason I tried it goes back about 50 years ago when I was a 14 year old, white girl, just confirmed in the Catholic Church. I had an experience that the Church could not answer. One minute I was myself, and the next I was a 6 year old black slave boy watching my grandfather working in the fields. The next minute, or however long it lasted, I was the 14 year old self I knew. Since I had no idea what had happened or what it meant, I didn't tell anyone about my experience, not even my best friend, Nancy. But, I never forgot it.

Five years later, I read the book, "The Search for Bridey Murphy", and then I had a name for my experience: reincarnation. I still didn't quite get it, so I started on a journey to understand what millions of people throughout the world, except in the Western world where I live, already believe.

Off and on, I read whatever I could on the concept of reincarnation, as well as other spiritual writings. Then the day came, in 1971, when I was at a wedding in a church and suddenly I felt faint. Having fainted a couple of times in my life, I got the thought that I wanted to see where you go when you faint. I shot through a tunnel to the top of the church ceiling, into a brightly lighted place where a man stood in a light gray monk type garment. I could also look down and see myself slumped over in the church pew.

This man was talking to me, but I couldn't concentrate on his words, because I was too freaked out, thinking I was dying. I had read about near death experiences and the tunnel and the light were mentioned frequently. There were two reasons I didn't want to die: My daughter, Courtney, was only 19 months old and I didn't want to leave her and, being a rather private person, I didn't want to die in front of a bunch of strangers at a wedding. I went up and down the tunnel a couple of times to this lighted place before I woke up in my body and ran to the bathroom, where I was sick. I did tell a few people about this incident, but when they asked me what this guy in the monk's robe had told me, I couldn't answer because I couldn't remember. I prayed that someday I'd know.

In the meantime, I continued on my spiritual search and joined groups like Self Realization Fellowship and Eckankar. I read books by Edgar Cayce, Raymond Moody and Jane Roberts. Then I read a book by Ruth Montgomery, who channeled her books about the afterlife through automatic writing. That sounded interesting to me, but I never attempted it myself. One day, many years later, I decided to try. It took about a week of sitting with a pen and paper and waiting. Then the pen started to move and a story of four of my past lives emerged for the next year. It was quite interesting. The monk from my out of body church travels, who spoke through those writings, said his name was Zian and he was my guide in this life.

One thing I've noticed when I've done automatic writing is that what is written today, I will often either read or hear the same or similar words within the next few days. I believe it's a confirmation, but also because these words are not a foreign concept, but a reminder of universal truths. The auto writings that came through Zian thirty years ago were mainly discussing and describing four of my past lives. But, the thread running through all the writings was about love as the most important reason why we exist and who we truly are.

When my mother was dying of pancreatic cancer in 1999, and before she went into a coma, she motioned to the beautiful light beings that she saw in her hospital room and one of the last things she said to me, in an amazed yet conclusive way was: "Oh, I get it, it's all about love and family."

My daughter was a writer at heart and she wrote a poem, which was even published in the prison news a few years later, about an experience she had with her son, Bleu, when he was four years old. She had her own apartment for a short time when she had gotten out of rehab and a halfway house and was clean. Or so we thought. I allowed her son to spend the night one weekend. She always said this poem would be the beginning of the book she was going to write. And it is, because THIS is the book she is writing.

The poem:

"Conversations Through the Bathroom Door"

"Mommy, the VCR won't play."
"Well, Baby, is the power on?"
Boy: "What color do I push?"
"The red button, and then it'll turn green, ok?"
"Well, can you just show me, Mom?"
"Not right now–Please–Just a minute, Honey."
…He's 4 years old, forever waiting for me to come out.
I pray to find a vein, but I can't see for the sickness.
My eyes water and my insides churn like butter.
My ears are ringing and I forget he's even there.
"I can't find my new book!! Where is it, Mama?"
"Look under the bed, Sweetie."
"No! Just come out now, Mom—I need you to look, too."
…He's pounding on the door now and soon
It'll turn into a rhythm that I can't even hear.
I finally flash and find my friend—in my neck—
Not hearing his pounding or questions.
I'm in heaven and my senses once again tingle
And I hear his voice again.
"Mom, are you coming? Mommy, are you okay?"
…I'll never know if he was watching.
I'll never know what my deafness did to him.
If only I could open that door the minute he asked for
help…
If only I could've pressed the play button…
But those are memories I now live with…
It doesn't stop me from wondering just what he saw…
Through the bathroom door.

A poem Courtney wrote for me around 2002:

You've never forgotten who I really am, and you had the patience while my memory was on the lam. You lent me your strength when I was cold and weak. You gave me your words of kindness when I could no longer speak. You showed me that beauty lies within me –You lent me your eyes when I'd forget to see. Thank You for noticing the spark I'd forgotten. No longer wanting—and life looks so much more clear—The One True Thing that is Love has brought me back to here.

I love you,

Courtney

Note: I might be able to do automatic writing, but I'm not a writer. The way it works is that I sit down with a pen and paper, and sometimes I'll get part of a thought, then the writing will begin. Sometimes, I will have no clue what is going to be written. Very infrequently, I'm able to type the messages, but regardless, the writing comes out in a stream of words with no capitalization or punctuation. I have tried my best to punctuate properly, but since I don't have an editor, I apologize now for any grammatical errors you may find while reading Courtney's writings. I think you'll see how the writings have evolved over the year. And, you may be able to see from the poem she wrote me years before her passing, that she had a spiritual knowledge she could express, but couldn't fully live.

The Writings Begin: Dec 18, 2010

Courtney—look back on past what good I did and what I didn't do—feeling much better now all is clear don't only think about what might have been—it was what it was—hard life. Not now, what is done is done, but what's important is know it doesn't really matter because I'm still here and doing what we always been doing: loving. We're really unchanging in our love. My love is like a continuous fountain that just got stopped up for awhile and flows now again, but was never gone. Love Courtney. Love you , love to Bleu and all. More later.

Dec 22

Mom—Ok you are doing well and I am doing great. Thank you for helping me to cross over. You are right about feeling like I came home. I had such a hard time on earth–that plane called earth and life, but this is life for me, not that, unless you are evolved enough to know what is going on there. All of us love life here. At first it's not so easy because you do see your whole life and what you've messed up and what you did good too, but the mess-ups are hard to look at and I slept for awhile at first but that was okay too. There was energy of people who helped me wake up and go through my life but no judgment from them, just like holding me up and surrounding me with love and non-judgment. What a relief. I took things so seriously, so sensitive, what a waste of time that is. Go lightly through the world was an excellent quote and so true. It's a game and a school and an observation, but it's not really life. This is life. I was way more dead there than here. Tell Bleu I love him and to laugh at life there and have fun, real fun, not serious. He's so wonderful and learning so much with you. Keep up the good work and thank you for being my guide when I'd let you be.

Once I woke up, I felt so strong I could open your computer. The cat got the candy cane off the tree and I placed it. I will try to show you more, but am getting busy. I'm doing more here than I did there. Will let you go and I love you.

(I asked Courtney for some signs that she was really still around and the next day I found my laptop open, which I'd closed and locked, and a candy cane on the kitchen table right at the place I always sit)

Dec 26

Bleu will be okay. He's such a good kid, let him be for now. I will keep allowing him to feel me in whatever way he can and I will visit him at night. If he can remember, it will be good for him. This life you are living is the illusion you've read about and have understood at times and it is the love that is real. All for now, love Courtney

Dec 27

The only home I'd ever known until now was with you. And don't take this wrong, but there is no home on earth that compares to the feeling of home here—it is all encompassing. There is a feeling of safety that nothing on earth can touch. You prayed that I would find a safe place while I was there AND I HAVE.

I love you, thank you for your prayers for me.

(I asked about putting an ad—the fourth one—to find a home for the cat, Remmie):

Answer: December thirty ad in at 5pm

(I did as she said and a woman called who had picked out another cat, but it fell through and she came over at the time Courtney said she would and Remmie found a good home with her)

Jan 3, 2011–Bleu's 12th birthday

Twelve years ago, I could have changed my life there, but I didn't. I don't know why I thought I couldn't. Basic immaturity, I think, too much responsibility, I think. It wasn't a lack of love for Bleu. I loved him greatly and I did try at first, but I also knew that you would take over the responsibility when I could no longer keep it up. He also knows that and why he came through me to you. Twelve years, forty years, sixty-four years—it's a blink of an eye just used on earth to keep some kind of order, but truly meaningless. Time is all now. All for now, love you all and always. Later on gab more Molly.

(Molly is one of our dogs)

Jan 4

Life can't be destroyed because energy can't be destroyed and we all have our own energy which is why we're recognizable to those who know us. This comes as a real shock to those who don't believe that there's more to life than on earth. I'm glad you always taught that there was more, because to some souls it can be traumatic for awhile to find out they're still alive after their body is gone. But they get over it eventually with a lot of help from both those on earth and those here.

Jan 6

Good morning and it is nice that you're receiving my messages in different ways and recognizing them as from me. *(I started writing down signs I was receiving from Courtney— from songs, to butterflies, to dream visits and more)* Yes, I will continue even if I'm busy here—that won't interfere with being there with all of you. Just keep being aware and you will know I'm here and there and it's all the same.

I visit Molly* (my 14 yr old dog who loved Courtney) at night. Share this with her because another month and she will be here with me.

(When Courtney was 13 we moved from Milwaukee to Birmingham, AL. When she was 17 we moved to Charlotte, NC. When she was 25, we moved to Denver. Courtney started traveling and ended up in Eugene, OR, where she got more and more into heroin and trouble. She called one day in 1997, not to ask for money, which she did regularly, but to ask to come to Denver and get clean. For the first time ever, my husband, Richard, and I had a house to ourselves. Nine months earlier we had bought a house after our two younger daughters moved out. We were having a wonderful time, but when Courtney called, I said yes, she could come and stay with us for six months and we would support her getting clean.

She arrived in Denver on July 4, 1997. After seeing our house for a minute, she asked to go to the hospital to treat an awful abscess she had on her upper right arm. They kept her for surgery and she stayed in the hospital on a morphine drip for three days. She was happy. A couple weeks later, a dog appeared at our door – a husky, shepherd, collie mix. She immediately fell in love with Courtney and we named her Molly, after no one claimed her. She slept with Courtney every night.)

Jan 7

I can't believe I hid myself from myself and everyone else for so long. I was a kind and fun person until I started doing drugs and then believed I couldn't live without them. It was that belief that did me in. I'm so glad that's over and that I can help others in the same situation and keep growing and learning and helping here, which is what I wanted to do there. How freeing this has been. Beliefs really are lies many times, but they're the first step to knowing. You don't have to hang on to beliefs that are no longer needed, but they are important to temporarily ground you until you know more. It's the negative beliefs you hang on to and let run your life and relationships and stop up the love that should be flowing all the time. That's why it doesn't matter what you eat, drink, etc. It's your belief about it that makes it real for you and when a lot of people have the same beliefs about one thing then it becomes a consensus and appears to be a truth. People get herded into "truths" that aren't even true and that's why you always need to look within for the truth for you and until you can touch that truth within you'll know it's just a belief.

So you don't get the idea that nothing you do can affect or ruin your body, since I'm a good example of that, not all bodies are the same and you have to know what your body can and cannot tolerate. It needs to come from within, not from so-called experts. In my case, the destruction came in my belief that I needed to take drugs to function. And like driving your car repeatedly into the side of your garage and not expecting to eventually hurt your car and garage, I thought I could keep doing drugs and not keep injuring my body. And even when I realized I couldn't, I still believed I needed them to function. And then my body, like any material thing, couldn't take any more. There are laws on earth and you must abide by some of them like breathing and eating and drinking and gravity, but the laws of what should and shouldn't eat or drink or even breathe are man-made and need to be decided for the individual body and your mind and spirit know what that is. Just wanted you to know it's about beliefs versus knowing. Okay, done for now.

You want to know how my leaving was. All I know is it was hard at first and got easier and easier. The hard part was allowing it to happen. Once I did, and you all helped me with that, then it got easier. I stayed close for the two days you were there, but toward the end I floated in a foggy place and then I left. The fog would part sometimes and I'd see the light and people I knew and then it was like falling back to sleep and waking up and sleep and waking and then I woke up and these energies were there helping and then I saw people I did know like *Nana and Grandma Burns and Steve and Grandpa Burns*, who I knew from before I came to you. Garv showed up and so did Bear and other pets we had, but they didn't all stay. Just came to say hello. The transition isn't scary once you allow. It's like being born, but since I was in such a drugged state, it just took a little longer to become aware of my surroundings. That's why babies, when you were born, didn't respond as well as babies whose mothers didn't have drugs before they gave birth. Same thing—mirror experiences—except when you're born there you start forgetting here and when you're born here, you start remembering what you really are and why you ever were born there. You forget why you went and now you remember why you did. Funny. Of course, the idea is to remember while you are there and then celebrate coming home when you're done. Mission Accomplished. Not an easy thing to actually do, but that's the goal and that's why people keep going back to try again. But, don't worry; I'm not going back anytime soon. That life kicked my ass. More later, I love you.

(She's talking about my mother, father, brother and grandmother —all who have passed on)

Few things want to say. First of all, when you're fully "here" and look at the life you had "there", you see that you were never a victim of anything. You are always a participant through the energy you're sending out which draws like energy to you. Change your energy through your thoughts and you really can change the course of your life despite what you might have set up for your life. Second of all, even if I decided to go back to earth before you pass, I would still be here too. Our highest real self is always in this plane, but it's where our focus is that makes it physical or non-physical. Do you see? We never completely leave our essential being because that's who we really are. We can't truly be something we aren't.

Jan 16

Beliefs are why Jews were killed, beliefs are why blacks were lynched, beliefs are why Indians were massacred, beliefs are why Mexicans are being deported, beliefs, beliefs, beliefs. I can't talk about this enough because beliefs are not knowing, they're lies we tell ourselves. Even addiction is no more than a belief—it is all in the mind where the belief lies. And it is a lie, it's never a truth. Only the truth can stop the insanity that lives on earth in people's minds and it starts with beliefs—negative, separating beliefs that keep people imprisoned there. It's so simple it's almost funny. It's not like anything is truly changed by beliefs because nothing can change the truth of who we are. Beliefs are a guide leading toward the truth or away from the truth, but beliefs are not the truth. It's really important to know and remember this. So sorry if I'm repeating myself, but it needs repeating over and over again.

There is no hell, but you already know that and there is no evil, only sickness, only a turning away from the truth and there is no death, all of those things are an illusion created in our minds when we think we're separate from other things. You already believe these things, but don't yet really know them, but you will and that is a lot of freedom to know these things. Freedom from worry, guilt, stress, fears—those don't exist with knowledge of the truth of what we really are. The physical body could live a lot longer with this knowledge, but right now the physical world is meant to be a playground and schoolhouse to visit for awhile. It's susceptible to deterioration and renewal and deterioration and renewal and on and on. The swings at a playground are a good metaphor for life: up and down, high and low and after so much you need to go home and rest and do other things. I'm re-learning a lot. These are all things each of us know and forget and re-learn. We remember when we're born, but then we have to learn society's ways and that really messes with our memories of what is and there we go—getting off course. Even when we retain some knowledge, we become unsure of it especially when we see so much wrong in the world and start feeling helpless and emotional. It's about remembering as much as you can while you're there. I know I keep saying here and there like they're totally different places, which they're not, but it's easier to differentiate. I love you.

Jan 17

You wonder what people do or feel once they pass over here and see their previous life. It's not so much that we judge ourselves for our ignorant beliefs and mistakes; it's that we become aware—like a revelation—and that there is no judgment from ourselves or others—that's an ego thing. We do not take our egos with us. The ego is not even real; it's just a thought that has no basis in reality. It's just another illusionary belief. There I go again talking about beliefs, but it's important. Love you, and you did liberate me.

Jan 22

Sherstin's dream about soccer: I never felt as good as Sherstin *(My middle daughter)*. Of course, I never felt as good as a lot of people, but loved Sherstin and looked up to her and always wished I could have her look up to me. She stayed on her path and I veered right off mine. Tell her I love her.

Jan 24

Everyone's passing over is as individual as everyone's life. Everyone experiences their own way and sometimes surrendering is easier for some than it is for others.

Jan 27

I asked: (Would it have been better if we'd let the doctors do what they wanted with you? What would it have been like for you?)

(The doctors said she would probably end up in a nursing home for life and asked if we thought she would like that, since she was

unresponsive. The answer was no. They suggested she be taken off life support after finding her lungs and brain were filled with abscesses and she would probably live in a vegetative state. Then they changed their minds and wanted to keep giving her medicine for the next two weeks, just to see what might happen. Our family discussed this and knowing she also had Hepatitis C and would probably be in a state nursing home for life, decided taking her off life support would be the kindest thing. The idea of her being in a state nursing home scared me badly. I felt she would end up being abused and we wouldn't always be there to protect her).

It would have been a continuation of the life I'd been living, except worse in ways because I would have been imprisoned in a place and in my brain. It was not what I wanted or needed. There would have been no growth or redemption. It would have also made all of your lives harder than they already were. It was a no win situation. The doctors would have failed themselves as well as the rest of us. I am glad to be freed of all of it and to know that all of you are freer too. It was the best ending for the path I took. There was no longer a turning back or going forward. I had literally ruined my body and it would have been a living death more than it already was. Thank you for caring enough to let me go.

I asked: (Is it time to let Molly, our dog, go?)

It's getting very close.

(Do I have to do it?)

Yes, and you'll know when. The third of next week.

(I had been watching Molly for a sign and when I got it, I realized Courtney was right— it was time to let her go. Bleu and I took her to the vet on February 3rd. She looked into my eyes and a second later was gone.)

Feb 4

Molly looked at you and the next thing she knew, she was here with me feeling young again. She's doing good, really good.

Everything here is based on energy. It's true there too, but it's not as obvious. It can be covered up by all sorts of outer pictures. It's hard to explain. Just like in your mind you can be other places: past, present, future—on an island using your imagination to travel—using your fear or worry to project into the future, using memory to go to the past, although the memory is usually tainted by emotion. Some days you wake up and you have more energy than other days. It's the same here. Energy fluctuates, focus can fluctuate, so although we can be in more than one place at a time, it also depends on our own energy and it takes a lot of energy to show you signs. It takes focus. So while we can be here and there and everywhere, it's not always easy to give a hundred percent to all those places.

When there are big earth events it draws our attention as it does yours, although we see it differently and don't get drawn up in the emotion of it. It's not all of us that are drawn, but many, many, especially those of us who are in rescue work and want to help those who are crossing over. And I'm still learning.

Most of my energy has been on that, and the stress you've been feeling does interfere or block your receiving, but do know I'm around and so is everyone you've ever loved or helped. Focus plus feeling plus energy manifests on earth as it is in heaven. Thoughts plus imagination allow for activity to become an experience of reality. This is an example of REALLY deep thoughts. HA HA HA. Molly is fine and happy. We'll talk about animals another time.

(There was an author/comedian who wrote about "deep thoughts" and Courtney and her sisters would make up their own, which were quite funny)

Feb 9

Let it be: remember everything happens in perfect time— use that as a mantra and affirmation. It will get rid of a lot of worry and stress. Nothing happens before the right time. That is a good way to live your life and to teach others to live theirs. That way you don't interfere with the natural order of the unfolding of your life. Of course, I didn't learn that, but I want you to. It will get easier, because I will keep reminding you, okay? There's nothing this can't help with—nothing.

Relax and allow—don't push for things to happen, especially when it doesn't feel right. That was a specialty of mine. But it wasn't like I was trying to make anything happen by action; it just stayed in my mind and drove me nuts. I'm just telling you this because I'm now aware, and to help anyone who does the same things. Allow everything in its perfect time. Live, love, laugh.

Feb 14

Time is a paradox and one you'll understand, but I can't tell you because it's something each of us needs to find for ourselves. It is important and it's not important. All time is now and everything happens in its perfect time. See— a paradox. You were told once that you would eventually find paradoxes inconsequential and amusing. In other words, you would be able to just accept them rather than try to dissect them. Get it?

What we do that keeps us busy. That's also individual and collective. Another paradox, but we are drawn to things here as we are there. And what we didn't accomplish on earth that we set up to accomplish, we are able to do here, or not. We always have some freedom to choose, but mainly we do things here that will help us grow further. There is more a sense of unity and cooperation because there is no ego; everything is for the benefit of all and that includes the people who are still on the earth plane.

Without a physical body there is only mind (soul) and spirit. Inspiration comes from here, imagination comes from here, innovation comes from here, and ideas come from here. Mind and spirit equal energy. Energy is all there really is and can be expressed in ways unimaginable for you right now and for me. It's not like I know everything already and it's not like it's not all here to know—so many paradoxes. It's an awakening upon awakening. Awareness is the first step to awakening. The more aware, the more awakened; the more awakened, the closer to knowing; the more knowing, not believing but knowing, the closer to truth; the closer to truth, the closer to peace; the closer to peace, the closer to atonement— at-one-ment. And then you know what "all time is now" means.

Feb 15

Heaven is a state of mind—it's not a place. And it's easier to glimpse that state of mind here more often because there is no ego which can continually get in the way of experiencing it there. There is a difference between places and planes of consciousness. You don't pass over and immediately wake up to the highest state of consciousness and you can stop on whatever plane you want for as long as you want. It's a remembering, remember? Just like on earth. It can be like a lotus flower opening —awakening slowly to the sun. You go to the plane that you can operate on and then the desire to move on and open up drives you to the next higher plane. You can rest for as long as you need to on the lower planes. You can make your life here a facsimile of your life before and you can do that for as long as you feel a need to. But eventually you'll be drawn to do more and remember more. Awakening further consciousness doesn't pull us further away from those we love; it expands your love to include more and more.

The plane I'm on is wonderful, but it doesn't mean I'm all-knowing. There is more remembering to do, more knowing to open to. It's all quite an adventure and quite an experience. And it can be done on earth, it's just harder, but worthwhile. The more awakened on earth, the easier here; the more awakened here, the higher the plane you get to go to. Or should I say arrive at. It really does matter how you live your life on earth and I'm not talking about your beliefs about what you should do to live a clean and healthy life. I'm talking about a growing of your consciousness—an opening—a oneness—a love for all, which is all there is, and all we really are.

Thinking your way is better than another's is not love; it's judgment and that comes from ego, not spirit. Find your way and allow others to find theirs. We're really just on a path to remember who we really are. That's all for now. I Love you.

Feb 18

("*Happy Birthday, Courtney. Forty-one years ago today, you came to earth through me and to me. I will never forget looking at you and you staring right at me, which was startling to me, because I thought all babies had their eyes closed at first. I said to you "where do we know each other from?" or "we've been together before" or something like that. It's hard to remember exactly.*)

And, yes, we had met before, many times. I see now how you loved and protected me as well as times you resented me and all of it is okay. And, of course, we'll be together again. I've lived quite a few lives cut short because it was so hard to stay. But, not always, sometimes I made it through to old age.

Every life we come to learn and to teach—sometimes more of one than the other. But we pick parents who have what we need to learn and to help us be more of ourselves, whether for or against their teachings. And a child always shows the parent who their parents are, whether negative or positive. It's about becoming aware of ourselves: the good, the bad, the beautiful, and the ugly.

Drugs interfere with the natural order of these things, but they don't stop it altogether. Drugs interfere with the learning of the addict, but not the parent—or child of a drug addict— and include alcoholics—same thing.

Feb 22

I asked: ("*What about children dying?*")

Well, you have to understand the child is not a child. It's a soul who went into a body to do a job, which is to teach and to learn and the time it took to do that varies. But, also, you want to remember that the soul who went and came back quickly has not had years of earth life to interfere with its remembering so the passing is not a shock or unfamiliar. It's more like going to school for a few days and returning home. The soul who has left doesn't experience sadness, but can experience empathy for those who are feeling the loss. Also, there is a reuniting with those on this side who saw the soul off and now are welcoming it back.

The one thing you need to remember is that children are just what are called children when they're in a physical body and the less they've forgotten; the easier it is to come over here. It's those who have forgotten that can have a harder time and that's usually what are called adults.

Also, we can appear whatever age is easiest to be recognized, but we naturally look in our 30's in the bodies we use here. But it is a matter of perception and I have to stop here because it sounds more complicated than it is.

Feb 23

(Bleu told me this morning that he had a dream about his mom. He said—Now, I finally know what you mean when you talked about drug addicts and how they're not their real self, because my mom was different in my dream. She was more mature and responsible. He could see the difference between who she really is and the drug addicted person he'd known. I told him I didn't think he had a dream about his mom, but a visit.)

March 4

I asked: ("What was with Bleu this morning?")

Bleu is going through some of the anger that you are too, and doesn't really know what he's mad at, but is going to take it out on you a little bit. Don't worry, but you can try to talk to him and let him know it's okay to feel that way. It's hard for him to admit anger at me right now, so it gets deflected back to you. It's just the same with you.

I asked: ("So where were you on Tuesday?")

(Although, my parents, grandparents, great aunts and my only brother had all passed on, I had never before contacted a medium. Because of some "coincidences" that had happened since Courtney had passed, I called a medium named Ocallah, to see if Courtney would come through. The medium had absolutely no knowledge of whom I might be trying to contact. Although, she gave me vague descriptions of my parents and brother, she only gave me a very vague reference to someone on drugs. Since she wasn't really getting much, she offered to try again in about six weeks or so. I did tell her then that the person I'd wanted to contact had passed over two months before. She thought it might just be too soon for that person to come through.)

It was hard to get through. There was a gathering around, but no one stood out, just trying to make some impressions and I'm not that good at this yet. Energy comes in spurts because of different focuses being split. It can feel like it's dissipating. It's hard to describe. Dissipating is not the right word, not fragmenting, but like crystal like.

(I could picture what was meant, but couldn't get a good word or description. I don't always understand what she's talking about.)

March 6

As I've told you, time is a paradox. To you, I've been gone for three months. To me, it's like one second and eternity. Isn't that funny? And so hard to describe. There are a lot of things that are hard to describe, not because I can't, but because it's hard for you to comprehend right now. But, you'll get it—you'll remember.

To answer your question and Nancy's *(my best friend)* about people waking up here and discovering that their beliefs on earth aren't true: like we said, it's all individual. At first, no, they're not shocked to find that they've had beliefs that weren't true. They knew unconsciously all along because their beliefs didn't provide them with love and happiness or a sense of peace. What they remember here is that none of their beliefs really matter in the whole scheme of things and that humans take on roles to help awaken themselves and others. If their role is to be a bigoted asshole, it is to make other's aware of the separation they're creating, which is not what life is for. And hopefully they recognize that while they're still on earth. Some people do and some don't: the ones that do find **life** on earth; the ones who don't never really live. Their intolerance and hatred become their death, not physical death, just an unhappiness that stays with them all their days, because hate is not a natural state of being. When we go against our natural state of being, we can't find love and peace. So these people can help others awaken to love as well as themselves. They have a role to play. If they finish that role without finding love and unity and peace, they remember it here, work on it here, and have a chance to try again. But don't judge those who hate, they just aren't remembering and they will awaken someone or many others even if they don't awaken themselves while they're on earth. We're all awake, we just haven't remembered yet.

March 11, 2011

Good morning. You really never have to worry about other people and their beliefs. You are there to teach and so are they. If someone believes something you don't and you judge them for it, you're only hurting yourself. Like I've said, beliefs aren't knowing—beliefs are transitory and temporary, they're not real and they run the world. There isn't one war or one dream or one achievement or one failure that didn't start with a belief since earth and physical experience is based on duality. Beliefs can either benefit or destroy. There're always two sides to a coin and a coin is a material, physical thing. Duality is just a way to learn on earth and to teach each other and yourselves about yourselves. It serves a purpose. But duality itself isn't real.

Once you know that, like paradoxes, you'll find duality inconsequential and amusing.

March 16

Earth is talking back. It can only take so much abuse until it rises up and gets your attention. The earth is a living thing, not stagnant. It's always expanding and contracting and changing, but the devastation is seen when people go beyond their capabilities to control their inventions and get greedy and egotistical and want to win at all costs. It's all part of the awakening—the fall before the rise.

The awakening has been going on since the original fall. Adam and Eve are symbols of that. The fall was because of the rise of the ego and seeing everyone as separate, without unity. The most recent widespread awakening began in the nineteen sixties and it has been slowly leading to now. Although it doesn't seem like it now, it will be hardest for those that have the biggest egos and the least empathy. But, it's okay. They'll someday remember, as we all will, that love and unity is what it's all about.

March 22

Ego is the real illusion because it's not real. It's made up to keep the illusion of separation and when you hear of someone with a big ego, that's the saddest thing that can be said about them, because they've missed the whole point of the experience of life in the physical world. They are sad underneath, but remember the ego can't last forever and it doesn't. Eventually, you can literally see the light that pushes you on. The ego is as temporary as the physical body and so are beliefs. Just ask yourself how many beliefs you've had in this life. How many do you still believe? How many have you kept, but they've changed?

Although believing is not knowing, some serve a great purpose in your life and those can be nurtured and lead to a positive way of living. Beliefs that lead to the experience of unity are the ones to keep until there is no doubt. Beliefs always come with some doubt about their reality, just as you've heard excitement always comes with some anxiety. Even an experience can have doubts attached after the experience. You certainly know that, right? It's all a part of life on earth.

Even as you're experiencing this communication, you wonder if it's really me. We're connected on deep, deep levels, so it is us together.

March 27

You can do here what you did there and many souls do for awhile. You can also try to live vicariously through people still on earth, but eventually you become compelled to move on with your remembering. You can experience all the pleasures here as you did before or even all the horrors, but it is not eternal. Eventually you literally see the light that pushes you on.

I said we can be in more than one place at a time and it's true, but isn't always the best idea. Focus matters. For awhile my focus was to let you know I was okay and still with you. Now it's more like drop-bys because the more focus, the better I get at other things to do here. Don't worry, we don't desert you and we don't move away as much as we move on for periods of what seems like time to you. And, you also aren't available every minute of your day. It happens when all the things are perfect for everyone involved.

April 4

(I asked about a hearing problem I'd had for about a month)

It is temporary and it will pass between this week and next.
(It did!)

(I asked about Autism)

Autism is a sign of the times reflecting technology and socialization or lack of. People with autism are here to teach others to love in a different way. Meaning they need love and they need to learn how to give love in a disconnected society that is isolating itself. They just depend more on others to show them the way. All epidemic type things are souls going together to teach a lesson the world needs to learn. These particular souls are caught in between here and there. Later.

(I asked about predestination vs. free will)

It's a combination between the two for every life on earth. Before you go to be born on earth, you do have meetings with other souls about what the meaning of your life on earth will be. It's not so much a plan as a blueprint or map. Not every minute is decided on, just a general map. On the map are certain people and destinations and challenges and opportunities and crossroads and those are where you make choices through intuition—or remembering what your map is—or you use your free will to take you in a different direction, which is okay, too.

There's a difference between being willful and being willing, and your gut can tell you that if you listen. I wanted to experience the wild side and see what darkness meant. I just didn't know I wouldn't be able to just stop when I wanted. Willpower doesn't do it, but willingness can and I never could get to that point. I certainly wasn't predestined to die a drug addict, but I was destined to become one and overcome it. But, I did too much damage to my body to pull it off—that wasn't predestined, but it was a likely conclusion if I didn't use some free will to say I choose not to continue and focused on that. I was too afraid of change to change my mind and you can see how that turned out. Actually, pretty good now, but it's not the way to go, because I gave up on life and love and that's the opposite of what earth life is for.

An addict lives a selfish life as though they're the only person that matters. The fix is the only thing that matters and it's a deadly and deadening cycle. You literally can't give much of anything to anyone else. You stop knowing what love really is and you really don't love yourself—there's no radiating love that can touch others and lift them up. But it's an experience I don't want to repeat. Heaven and hell aren't places, but they can be experienced and everyone does in their own way. Except when you wake up and realize both are in your mind and in your map and in your choices and what you want to experience.

What's funny is that none of it really changes your essential spirit—your spirit remains intact and your soul remembers more with each passing.

April 8

Now it seems to people that how can this be if we don't have a body that we can still be living, but we do have a body here it's just not a physical body. Just as you can sense energy and see the results of energy, you don't see energy. It is the force behind all things and when it's harnessed you see the result. So, if you see us, it's because we're harnessing the energy we're all made of to show you something. It depends on where you are whether you can see it or sense it or hear or feel the energy of someone who's left the physical body.

It's very much like taking off your clothes especially clothes that don't fit very well, and underneath there is your body. When we die we take off the body and underneath is another body—not heavy or uncomfortable, but light and airy. It really doesn't seem like it should be so hard to understand that, but the physical world draws you in so completely that it seems like the only reality there could possibly be. But within everyone is a memory of what was and is. That's why religions were started—to try to help people remember. But when spirit combines with the ego, there are problems. Then the memory that we all possess becomes messed up with 'my memory is better than yours' and 'I know the real truth and you don't' and on and on until people are fighting about their essential selves whom they no longer remember. And love is lost for that time until someone wakes up and knows the memory is about energy and love. Many people remember it on their way out, like your mother did. The key is to remember it throughout your life there and you can, at least in moments when the ego is forgotten. And, of course, there are some people who do remember like Buddha and Jesus, but then people who understood their truth got involved with following them and starting religions and interpreting and misinterpreting and instead of following and making the truth theirs, they began to lead before knowing how to live the truth and bumping against others who were doing the same thing all based on beliefs, instead of real knowing within them. None of it changed the essential truth of what really is.

The physical body was never meant to last forever. It's just to wear for awhile while you experience the earth. It's only the ego that gets attached to it so it seems that you will cease to exist without it. Not true. You can't cease to exist. The ego is what causes you to doubt and keeps you attached to these beliefs that anyone could actually die. You exist now and forever. It can't be otherwise.

April 9

Before you're born you make kind of like a bucket list of things you want to do and experience before you move on back to here, where you look at what you wanted to do and you did based on your choices. Some things are set, some things are flexible. Your ancestors and parents are set, usually because you have something to learn from them and always because you have something to teach them. Sometimes there is no history with the family you choose for different reasons. Either because the soul jumped the gun or they wanted to learn independence or because they need to learn to love others unlike them. But usually if the time has been taken here to make your list, you'll choose a family of souls you've known before and have things to either work out or expand upon—like a continuation of the relationship. It can always be a detriment or a growth, the underlying reason is to grow and experience love between the souls to help each remember the truth of love.

So, you have this path that you decided on and you're carrying your bucket of things you want to experience. The path is never straight on earth and there are always crossroads where you can go left or right and that's where intuition is useful, but the ego always wants to make things more complicated by trying to be rational in its decisions, which are usually based on unconscious beliefs about yourself . To rationalize is the ego's trademark.

So, you get to this crossroad and you intuitively know which way to go, but the ego starts doubting and confusing the issue and sometimes you choose right and sometimes you take a path that doesn't fit your to-do list and the way you know is because how it makes you feel. If it doesn't make you feel good, you will always get to another crossroad where you can choose again. Even if you're in prison for life, there will always be crossroads. Because even if it looks like you're now on one path, you can change your mind about how you see it, see yourself and the others. All for now.

(I asked about jumping the gun before a soul is really ready.)

Some souls want to jump back into a physical body because they want to finish what they started or do a better job or for whatever reason. They don't take the time to do the work here—to remember—and work with their guides to map out their next life or even if it's a good fit and they'll just jump right in. Then they'll have to decide if they're going to stay or come back here as quickly as they can. Many times the reasons very young children and babies die or seem to. Planning a new life is not usually a solitary venture. Sometimes people come back quickly because it had been such a good fit, but mostly we take our "time".

Anyway, crossroads sometimes have exits which sometimes you can take and sometimes it's just a wake-up call and you're sent back to continue on your path with your still to-do list. And it usually does turn into a wakeup call. These are the near-death experiences that people talk about. People who remember the experience rarely go back to complete ignorance of life after the earth life. Most never fear death again, because they know. An out-of-body experience is somewhat different which is what you had in the church. I will talk about that another time. I love you and thanks for being there—or here.

April 16

Out of body experiences usually happen in one of two ways: through deep meditation or what seems spontaneous, which you had. They can also happen when you're sleeping. The difference between out of body experiences and near death experiences is basically one: your body is shutting down, where out of body experiences are not life threatening and there is no decision to stay or go back to your body. You are going back, because you're not dying; and as with actual passing over, every experience is individual.

You've heard the expression, especially with babies or very young children, especially with SIDS, that they were called home to God or heaven. And it's kind of true, but it's a two-way call between the soul and here with their guides and angels. The decision is made together to stay or go. It's like a combination of an out of body and near death experience. They leave with the intention of not going back even though their body isn't sick. Their body shuts down when they leave. Understand? That's why they still can't figure out how SIDS happens. But they'll, of course, keep looking and speculating the cause of it. We all have an exit early on if we want to take it. The soul knows. Have a good day.

April 20

I said:

(Wow, Courtney, yesterday was great. I'm so glad you were able to come through. I had my second session with Ocallah— www. ocallah.com —and Courtney came through very strong. My great-aunt T Daw came through first. The medium didn't know anything about Courtney or anyone in my family. These are some of my notes from my session with the medium.

She mentioned a house near the beach that my grandmother and mother—both deceased—didn't want to give up. I realized it was the house I'd grown up in and owned by my great aunt, T Daw— short for Auntie Adele. The medium, Ocallah, kept naming names that didn't make sense and said she was going to stop with the names, but there was one more that she just had to say because it was unusual. She said Adele. That blew me away! She went on to describe her and things she did in life so I knew it was her. T Daw told her there would be a baby girl coming into our family and that would be her. I found out a week later that my youngest daughter, Brecken, was very unexpectedly pregnant and it will be a girl due in December, 2011.

T Daw said I was writing a book of channeled writings from my family. I guess this is it! Then, abruptly, the medium said Life Support and I knew this person so well— my daughter. She mentioned brain infection and brain swelling and that she was an addict. She mentioned heroin. I had not told her anything about anyone I wanted to connect with. Ocallah said she—Courtney—

was with people helping to lift the veil. The session ended with Courtney showing the medium a purple flower. I was hoping she would acknowledge her son who had bought her purple flowers for her birthday after her passing and I believe that she was acknowledging him.)

It's always wonderful to let you know I'm around and T Daw loved it too. Everyone was there. When I said look at only the light, I was talking about eliminating any fear or anger that the dark can produce in people. I wasn't talking about ignoring the bad news, but seeing it for what it is and that's an opportunity to turn it to good and not getting caught up with the desolation and despair that seems to be an appropriate response, but is really just a paralyzing reaction.

Your normal reaction is to look at the good, but with what's happening in the world and in the US, there's still a tendency to feel that there's nothing you can do and maybe it's best to ignore. But keep signing your petitions and allowing the news to wake people up without being drawn down by it. It's the time of awakening and people wake up when they become aware. It's a part of lifting the veil. For centuries the veil has been drawn tight and now it's beginning to lift so that there is light shining through. Now there's some light shining through to dispel some of the darkness. Remember the dark is just an absence of light. I love being a part of it and doing what I was unable to do when I was there because I was too immersed in the dark.

April 22

Dramatically speaking, the world is coming to an end. The earth is not, humanity is not, but the world you know is. And that doesn't mean your world, but things are coming to a head. Everyone on earth lives in a different world in their minds, but you all live on one earth. There really is a third world war going on right now. Just look around and you'll see all the uprising against the egotistic and the humanitarians who want to live in peace and freedom.

Let's talk about cooperation and competition since that's on your mind. Cooperation brings unity, competition brings separation. Seems pretty simple to just put it like that, doesn't it? But it's the truth. The places that deify competition are not faring so well, because truth is not on their side. Sometimes the line looks fine between cooperation and competition. There are those who cooperate to bring competition. There are those that compete to bring cooperation. Well, they don't always compete, and then some get drawn into the competition to do good or what they think is good, but that's getting complicated. What I'm trying to say is that true cooperation is for the common good. It's for love and unifying. Everyone has that as their base, but the ego wants to be better, best, which can only separate, which is the opposite of unity. I seem to be repeating myself and it's worth repeating. If you're going to compete, compete with yourself to bring yourself to a higher level.

There truly is an awakening going on and it will lead to a lot of squabbles and everyone is playing their roles right now. Many people will change their minds and those that don't will be left behind for awhile. Separateness is just an illusion. I should have written a song like that!

We can all feel your love when you send it to us. Love never dies – true love expands. Souls come together on earth for a purpose and there's always a lesson despite the amount of time they're together. Sometimes for a short time, other times for life. There's always something to learn and to remember. The veil is not always a heavy curtain, it can become very flimsy at times and seen through and for many it will happen more and more. Unite with me in lifting the veil. I love you.

April 24

Just want to let you know that Gabe was not my guardian angel, but my guide, as Zian is yours, or at least one of them. Gabe was with me all my life and was a human at one time who knew me in previous lives and took on the very hard job of trying to help me. But he never left me, and was here when I came over. He's still guiding me here for awhile and then he will be free to move on. If he goes back to earth, who knows, maybe I'll be one of his guides!

We all have a main guide and others who join in to help as much as we'll let them. The more open you are and the more you ask and attune yourself to the guidance, the easier life on earth can be. It's a form of lifting the veil. You even got a chance to meet Zian and he's still there with you. So don't forget him. You might remember that I also met Gabe a few times. If I would have listened to him the second time I met him, my life would have turned out much different. But there wouldn't have been the Bleu you know now. Everything does happen in its perfect time and in a right way even though choices could have changed it all and that would have been perfect too.

(When Courtney was about two years old she saw a green light. Other people saw it too. I told her that I thought it was her angel. We were all into doing the Ouija board at the time and this entity came through and said his name was Gabe and he was Courtney's guardian. When she first got into heroin at about 20 or 21 years old, she also got off of it by herself. She told me that during her withdrawal she had seen Gabe and he helped her through it. Unfortunately, she soon got back into heroin and although she never saw him again, she never forgot him.)

April 26

Lifting the veil is about the awakening. It can't be done without open minds and an attunement with your mind and soul. Awareness is very beneficial, but not always necessary. People can have spontaneous revelations and they will never be able to go back to believing that earth life is the only life.

First, passing over doesn't have to be through illness, but it's become that way, or through catastrophe or through war; it can be as simple as projecting yourself either way, which is how it once was. Is that really so hard to fathom?

Earth life, for most, is like falling in a hole and someone puts a board across the top and all you can see are the sides of the hole—no sky, no sun, no moon, no trees and on and on. Then someone comes along and moves the board and you can see the sky, the sun, the moon, but you're still stuck in the hole. Then someone else puts a rope or ladder in the hole and you climb free up into the light. And you can also climb back down; back and forth when you want. There are better analogies, but that's a simple one. We've all been up and down the ladder many times and it's ego that places the imaginary board over the top until you die. That's how it works for most people. But there are others who move the board and you're able to climb the ladder for short periods of time and know there's more than a hole you're stuck in. There are many more of you than there have been. The board represents the veil.

May 1

When I said, focus on the light, just the light *(through the medium)*, I don't mean not being aware of the dark. It means bringing light to the dark in a way that you can without getting angry or negative or over emotional. You don't have to take the dark into your body. You need to look, listen, act, and let go, not hang on to the negative feelings that come up when seeing the darkness. Not letting the feelings become a part of you or else they will turn on you. Use compassion, not anger, as a motivator when you find a cause you want to be part of. It can be all in the way you see it, whether it's done out of hate or love. When I say you, I don't mean just you, but people in general.

You just saw something on puppy mills that was disturbing. If you want to see puppy mills banned, then it has to be for the love of the dogs and their lives, not because you hate what the owners are doing to the dogs. You see the difference? One is for, one is against. Always do things for rather than against. The flow is different for there's a flow for; there's a flow against—there's a resistance and that causes a tension and an opposite resistance on the other side—like a tug of war. Being for is the light, against is the darkness and what you're for needs to be a positive; something that brings unity, not separation. It brings empathy and love, not abuse and carelessness. I hope I'm making this clear enough, because you can be for things that cause hurt to others, as puppy mill owners are and so many other things you're seeing today in the world. It's pretty simple really: for unity, compassion and love or for separation, abuse, and carelessness. Big difference. I could go on and on, but you get the point even if the word "for" is used.

May 2

So, what happened with bin Laden is a good example of what I was saying yesterday and before about being for and against, and especially about beliefs and how things can go out of control by things based on beliefs. And thinking if you believe it, it must be the truth. Bin Laden and his followers believed sincerely that the United States was the devil, as the U.S. believes he is the devil. Now much of the world is for his killing and many of the world are against it. And the world goes round and round.

Bin Laden will more than likely be in a deep sleep before he does a life review. But I can't say for sure, because I don't know him. His soul will need to be healed and that will take as long as it takes. His spirit is waiting.

May 5

There is always someone being persecuted on earth and for the one doing the persecuting, they usually think it's for that person's well being. The persecutor thinks they are a savior by telling that person how they should live their life in accordance with the persecutor's beliefs. It always goes back to beliefs and believing that the beliefs are truth for everyone.

Beliefs are lies we tell ourselves when we don't know the truth. Beliefs feel like a truth for the one believing them until they no longer make sense and another belief takes its place. Truth is truth and unchanging unlike beliefs that change as we evolve.

Like I said, I'm not at a level to remember or know everything, but that is the goal or destination for all souls. I continue to awaken here just as you do there. I just have a broader perspective now.

May 9

I am not Brecken's *(my youngest daughter)* baby to be. I can do more good here right now and want to. I've got so much more to learn and remember here before I go back to learn more there.

Before I go for now I want to say I tried to get through yesterday (Mother's Day), but your anxiousness blocked me, except for my name. *(I watched a show that night and there were not one, but two girls named Courtney in the show)* The veil is being lifted in many ways and one is telepathy.

May 10

Every soul's transition and experience of passing over is different depending on where you're at when you do. There are different levels of experience. As I said, I was in a foggy state for awhile and was able to move on to a better level because my intentions, even though I was unable to help others there and because I knew in my heart the spiritual aspect of earth life, even though I messed up my life doing drugs.

So, my transition from the fog to being able to help was not as hard as some souls who get stuck in the muck of their previous lives and stay stuck in a grayness of their minds because of the hate or unforgiveness they pass over with.

Life on earth is to grow and awaken to our true natures; to remember who we really are. This makes the transition to this life a lot easier. Remember your brother's transition was not joyful until he was able to communicate with you and then things here changed for him for the better. He couldn't accept the fact that he'd died and had no body to continue doing what he'd been doing on earth. It was very frustrating for him so he hung around lower levels to try to continue experiencing what he knew until he could see things differently. It's not much different from life on earth, where you're in a state of negativity. That state doesn't change until you are able to see things differently. Passing on or death really is a continuation. It's all life.

I said I would talk about pets, so I will. Pets are a projection of the humans who have them and they are a gift to yourself. They'll not only show you who you are, but also who you can become. They are simple and pure souls who want to please their people. They have emotions and feelings that can be nurtured or destroyed. Any abuse of an animal takes away from your own awakening, as does any abuse of another person. Kindness and empathy for all living creatures: animal, plant or human, even the earth, all leads to awakening whether you're on earth or here.

The veil is only a temporary mental block between there and here. Here it isn't a real physical veil and can be transcended the more awakened and aware you become. Kindness and empathy in all things lead to the light and rid darkness of its hold on the human race through the human mind where darkness manifests. To learn to love our neighbor is the reason we come back. It's our true purpose on earth.

May 17

It's much harder to love your neighbor—I don't mean just on your block—when you're in a physical form than it is here. When you're there, there are so many things that get in the way—mostly ego and beliefs that create learning opportunities, but usually end up being obstacles created by the ego and beliefs that often seem too hard to overcome.

It seems easier to fight and defend rather than overcome and forgive. So that's what usually happens—fights and wars and defense. Peace and love and forgiveness seem too hard, but those are the things that let a soul grow and reach a higher spiritual perspective. Then those qualities start drawing more and more positive results to your physical life. Like attracts like. Opposites attract only as a challenge to realize that like attracts like. When people are on the same page, they work together. When they're not, it creates friction and tension which can lead to defense and fights, depending on how highly evolved the people are.

I said: (You have two opportunities to come back, will you? The first opportunity was Brecken's baby and the second is Sherstin's. I was afraid that Courtney might come back before she was ready.)

As I've said, I will not be coming back for quite awhile. I need this time here to not only rest and grow—I still need to do that, but I also have the opportunity here to be who I was meant to be there; to be helpful, to do constructive things rather than destructive.

May 22

Beliefs are the cause of wars, but they are also the cause of accomplishments. Beliefs that cause accomplishment lead to knowing, obviously, because once you've achieved something, you know and experience it. The "act as if" is the first stage of believing that leads to achieving and to knowing. You don't always start out by believing something will happen or manifest, but with practice and repetition you begin to believe and the further you go in that you can see results.

There are obviously positive beliefs and negative beliefs and each of them can manifest depending on the depth of the belief. Negative beliefs will never lead to peace and unity and love. One thing every person is capable of doing is changing negative beliefs to positive beliefs. Whether they do or not is a matter of free will. It's a matter of not being willing to see things differently. Willingness is the first step to change. At first we don't succeed… We all have many tries to do it right.

May 25

There is already a world war on earth between the old and the new. I'm not just talking about generations of people with different beliefs, but those that want to turn back time; those who don't want to yield power to people they see as inferior or superior. It comes from insecurity in their underlying beliefs about God and earth and life, and the afterlife. They profess faith, but don't really have it. Real faith will lead you to know that life is unending and that all souls are made of spirit and all spirit is equal and loving and unchanging. Keep practicing only looking to the light.

On earth, birth is looked at as a beginning and death is seen as an ending. A birth is usually seen as a happy event, and death seen as sad, but it's all where your focus is—your perspective. When you're in a body, you think a new body is the greatest thing to welcome and when we're here we think the same when a person passes over to this side. It's all perspective. We just have a larger perspective because we can see both sides, and most humans can only see one side. That's where lifting the veil comes in so that all of us can see both sides and that life is continuous no matter where you are.

June 2

Life is wonderful if you let it be. One of the things that make it not is letting irritations get to you, especially when they pile up and become greater than their parts. If you can learn to overcome irritations, you can be much better prepared to handle bigger things that interrupt everyone's life at one time or another.

If you let what is just to be, your life path can be or at least seem to be smooth rather than fighting or resisting, which only makes the road rougher. When you get caught up in resistance, there is always suffering and when there is suffering there is unclear thinking. And when there is unclear thinking there are unclear actions. Clarity is important for positive actions and results. Clarity also helps you from getting scattered and overwhelmed, because then any accomplishment is hard to achieve. That's how I spent my life and all of it was just in my mind that controlled everything in my life. I thought at first that drugs would help that and they only made it worse. The more you can silence your thoughts, the more you can focus and the clearer you become and that's when you know how and when to act or not act.

Everyone can use these tips and these are especially for Bleu: my love letters to him and all of you.

June 6

It is so beautiful here. All the same things there can be found here because this is where they begin. It's just more vibrant here, more clear, because we don't have the burden of unconsciousness. The more conscious you become, the more vibrant your world becomes. It's true on earth as it is in heaven. Life on earth can be just as beautiful when you can see it. Earth life seems a struggle because of beliefs that have been taught and handed down about the human condition and the separation between people and God and heaven. In reality there's no separation at all, which seems so hard to believe that people just stick with the illusion they've been taught. Within, people know there's more than just what they see. That's why religions exist. Unfortunately, the religions have become so distorted that they are more of the problem than the solution and have made people believe in the separation of themselves from the source of themselves that's called God. There's no separation at all. We are all one with God and God with us: no separation—all one.

The ego is just the thought of separation that we think we need to protect ourselves from God's wrath and from others, but God has no wrath, because God is only love, nothing less, and so are we. People may cringe at that because they think they want God to be separate and superior and ultimately in charge, but the ego also wants to be in charge, so there always seems to be a conflict between humans and God that doesn't exist in reality. When there's the feeling of separation from God, there are the feelings of guilt and shame that can ruin your life experience, as it sure did mine.

The reason I didn't like the things that could have made me recover was because I didn't want to give up control to a higher power, because I didn't know a higher power. Even though you taught me about God and the spirit, it was all just an intellectual understanding for me that made sense, but never got to the feeling stage, because it felt like feeling would be too painful; that it would show how rotten I was, not how beautiful I was. And not how beautiful everyone and everything is. That's how it works for drug addicts, but not just drug addicts, but for most people who think God is anything other than love. Or that God is another, separate entity.

June 8

The awakening is happening for all those who become more and more conscious in their daily lives. Unconsciousness is what has kept people asleep for all these years and years of earth existence. And unconsciousness is how the ego likes it, because that's what keeps the ego alive and kicking. When you become conscious you are truly becoming your real self and that benefits everyone.

Reactions are unconscious. Responses can and usually come from a conscious decision and from a place of deep feeling and not an emotion. Those things are different. Think about it.

Thoughts are fleeting and emotions come from thoughts. But feelings are deeper and come from the soul, or often said to come from the heart. Emotions are instinctual; feelings are intuitive. Instincts are on more of the physical plane and intuition comes from beyond the physical senses. See the difference?

June 13

Remember there is no need to overcome the ego, because the ego is not real. The thing you can do with the ego is dismiss it, because the ego is not real. There's no reason to feel guilt or shame. No one actually has an ego, they have a thought that they're separate from God and others and that thought started from a metaphor that was misinterpreted and then taught over and over again so that it seemed to be part of the human condition and experience. It seems more real than God because so much attention is paid to it as a thing people possess, instead of a thought that's been perpetuated by the very thought that made it up. The ego's not a real part of anyone—not to be overcome, but dismissed.

June 14

Jesus was his name, Christ was his consciousness—it wasn't his last name. Or, you can say, it's everyone's last name, because Christ is the consciousness of who we really are, which Jesus came to teach and to show by his actions and to show that we all have the same consciousness because we all come from the same source. Christ consciousness is love consciousness. It's the only true consciousness which shows we are all one and distinct at the same time. He didn't come to start a religion, but to bring truth and the joy of who we are. Boy, has that gone wrong!

Ego consciousness is the thought that we can't all be one. That some are better and some are worse. Christians think Jesus is better than them and those who don't believe are worse than them, which is not what he taught, but has become a belief—with lie right in the middle of the word. And it causes pain to so many people, but it doesn't change the truth. Beliefs can never change what's true. Beliefs can get you started, but only true knowing can bring you home.

June 18

Before I get started, just let me say that all the stuff on politics will change, but not for awhile. People really will wake up to what's going on between the rich and the rest of the country, but it will take a sort of revolt by the people to keep standing up for what's in their own best interest. It first comes down to that before the light will shine for others. You are right that people, not all people, but most need to take a direct hit before they wake up to what's right for all.

Now, to go to what I wanted to talk about and that is being born and re-born and evolving and becoming enlightened, which is the true purpose of being born on earth and that doesn't happen in one lifetime on earth. Some, like Jesus, take a few rounds, but most of us need many more than that to get it right.

When the bible was changed to exclude reincarnation, it changed everything in the western world. Beliefs don't change truth. Will talk more about this, but that's how power can seem to change truth to go along with the powerful person's personal agenda. But the rich and powerful will be there until they die and then they will remember that abuse of power was not their first intention until they got caught up in it and will have a chance to try again. Power is only a fantasy lived on earth for awhile and although it seems very real to those on earth, it doesn't change anything that's true. That's why earth life is often called an illusion.

June 22

Everyone on earth lives in their own world and when you can find another person to share the same vision as you, you've found a soul mate. It doesn't have to be every vision, just most. It is not that much different here, but soul mates are easier to find without ego. There is a lot of support for your visions and imaginations. On earth, there is too much worry that fills your thoughts and takes away from actually seeing what's going on in front of you. That is how you live in your own world, because everyone's thoughts and worries and past influence their perceptions, and perceptions differ accordingly. They are filtered through thoughts and beliefs and baggage. That's why stilling the mind for even a second can bring revelations that transcend perceptions.

June 28

All negative emotions come from fear. It is underneath all of them. You can't have anger or hate without it and the fear is always of extinction or pain and suffering in some way or another. To be fearless is to really live. To be fearless is to really know reality, to know love. Fear is a thought brought on by the idea of separation. When you only know unity, you will never acknowledge fear as something great. God is the antithesis of fear and in reality, they both can't exist.

July 2

The way to remember that God is love and only love is to find that spark within yourself that knows the truth of that; to remind yourself as often as possible that not only is that truth a possibility, but a reality that will never change regardless of what you see or think or believe. And as you begin to feel the truth of God as only love, your thoughts, actions and beliefs will change to encompass that truth and your life will reflect back to you the truth of it.

Love is limitless and cannot be contained, as hard as people work at containing it. What you see is not about God, it's what people believe about God as an autocrat trying to control the world. There is no God of fear or vengeance or judgment or punishment. All of that is a man-made interpretation or misinterpretations, I should say. It's humans wanting to put responsibility on God for whatever happens in their lives that they've created with their own thoughts and beliefs.

We're not inferior beings under God; we're beings with God and just can't accept that we carry within us all the love God is. We need to remember that as truth and we will.

July 7

The day begins and ends with looking at the best possible ways to live your life through understanding of what you have learned and where you are and the joy of a new day and the way you can enjoy every minute of that new day. It is the best way to live on earth and what draws us back to living on earth: the rhythm of earth life, the surprises, even the obstacles are a draw for the soul to want to experience the roller coaster thrill of it, the drama and the comedy of it—the light and the dark and the seasons of life and the relationships that become our mirror.

Souls don't go back just to make amends, but to experience the three dimensional for a time without getting so caught up in it that they forget where they really came from. But most people do forget and then spend their lives seemingly enmeshed in situations of their own making and trying to get out, instead of enjoying the moment by moment experience that could bring them joy. There's no need to struggle or suffer on earth because whatever is happening can change with a change of mind and focus—just looking at the same thing in a different way.

If you don't like what you're seeing, look at it differently and it changes. If you do like what you're seeing, look at it differently and it changes. People do it all the time— everything is going along fine and then a thought comes and is latched on to and boom, it seems your life sucks. It works both ways. It seems harder to see the positive when you're seeing the negative, but it's just a matter of choice and desire. It seems easier to be a victim than a survivor—it's all in the way you look at it. A victim doesn't feel the need to take responsibility for their selves. A survivor knows they need to take responsibility to not live as a victim. I painted myself as a victim of insensitive kids and then became a target for the rest of my life and never had to take responsibility, because poor me. People are starting to see the difference between being a victim and being a survivor. That's good. It will change their whole life experience. Well, that's all for today. I love you.

July 8

I want you to understand that when I talk about my life as Courtney that I am not suffering from my choices, because I can look at it without emotions. Negative thoughts and emotions are what cause suffering. Without those, you can only observe without judgment. It's like reading a book about someone else's life without attachment.

July 14

When people you know arrive here you know them immediately. Not by their personality, which is often used to cover up your real self, but by the energy of their soul. Our true self is our spirit which is energy. Our spirit is where we all connect. Our soul is our individual expression of our spirit. Our soul carries our experiences and memories and uniqueness. Our personality is a persona we take on while on earth to accomplish our reason for being on earth, but it oftentimes covers up who we really are and becomes a projection of what we want other people to believe about us or what we've come to believe about ourselves. Personality is not the true self, but it can point to the true soul. On earth there are always layers to uncover to get to the truth.

July 21

Since ego is just a mistaken thought and not a reality, there is no more reason for you to have an ego there, anymore than here. But as long as you believe in separation, you will have the thought that creates the ego and makes it seem real and something to overcome instead of dismiss, when you become aware of it working in your life.

Life is not a journey of overcoming things, at least that's not the real purpose. Life is an awakening to what and who we really are. And we can awaken at any time in any life. Why not make it now and this life? Usually it's because we think we need challenges or to find our earthly purpose or because we like drama or feel the need to defend ourselves against our enemies or on and on, because it's hard to stop lifetimes of belief in the human condition. The idea of journeys, like so much in the human mind, there seems to be so much to overcome. But the truth is awakening is just remembering the truth of who we are. It can happen in a split second or as a process through one life or many—on this side or that side.

July 28

Good morning to you. There is a lot of interest here about what's happening on earth and in America. It will work out and Obama will be re-elected because people are waking up to what is happening. It's a cycle that continues throughout history. Remember the French Revolution; remember Rome and whenever the rich become too powerful and too rich at the expense of the average people. When the gap between the rich and the poor grows bigger and bigger, the people rise up and make changes because the people are always the majority. So when they become one out of many, they do much to create changes. Remember why unions were started— it's a replay.

Aug 1

There will be more and more found out about what's called the Tea Party and their deep connection to their religion. It's just another example of how beliefs can ruin other people's lives and start wars where there don't have to be any. It does make for good drama, doesn't it? High suspense: like a really scary mystery —people on the edge of their seats. The truth is humans love drama and thrillers and to be scared a little bit. It keeps the ego happy. It's part of the experience of earth life until you just really want peace and unity and fairness. It's coming, but not in your lifetime—maybe next.

This twenty first century is for awakening on a grand scale and it's become a process. The vibration is rising on the planet even if it doesn't seem like it on a daily basis or when you look at politics or what seems like natural disasters or man-made disasters. Duality is becoming more and more obvious so that people wake up to old thought and new thought. It's a time of change and transformation and all of you came to watch and participate in this now and to choose as individuals and collectively whether you're ready to move on. It's a great time to be on earth and great time to watch from the comfort of here and help as much as we can to help raise the vibe. All our love to you all.

Aug 8

As we said before, there is predestination and there is free will and both work together to make your life on earth. Affirmations work when they are in agreement with what you have chosen before your birth. But they also work because you want to see things differently when you've gotten off track; to pull you back into a more positive frame of mind which attracts positive or like vibrations to you. All the aspects of your affirmations may not always turn out exactly as you've affirmed them, because they might not be part of your pre-life arrangements. But the essence of the affirmations will be felt in your life.

For instance, if your affirmation is for a million dollars, the essence of the affirmation is for a feeling of security, where there is no reason to worry about money in your life and you will get what you need so as not to worry about money. You may not get a million dollars, but you will not be destitute either. Sometimes an affirmation is a remembering of what you pre-decided before this life, to have in this life, and it is beginning to be the time of that to arrive. The closer the results come to the words you're using to affirm, the more likely it is because you've remembered your pre-birth plans that are becoming manifest.

Whether you actually get what you affirm or you get the essence of what you affirm, it's always a positive result.

Aug 10

I am following the rules of assignments and loving it and am looking forward to continuing to move on and learn and grow and relax and love and have peace within and without. Just being surrounded by all of that and giving it, it's what we all want to experience on earth, but life on earth with an ego leads us to be confused and forgetful of what our true purpose for life is, whether here or there. It's just very pleasant here and I need that after the turmoil of my last life.

Aug 11

I'm still helping to lift the veil so that light can shine through more often for those on earth who can recognize and see it while still on earth, which helps when you cross over to this side. This is not a new thing and has been done at times in the history of the earth to lift the vibrations of those on earth. The book you're reading is not an accident, but so that you know that what we've been saying is the way things are. And as we said, there is only life and it goes on and it's never boring here, because there is so much to do for our individual souls and for all souls because one soul affects many souls because we all come from the same source and are one. One soul can do much, but many together can do even more when they're unified in purpose. On earth, that can be for negative or positive results. Here it is only for positive results of growth and learning and love. One for all and all for one is how it is when there are no egos, and to be strived for when you're on earth. Why wait?

Aug 12

There are many reasons you might choose a life that seems so hard. Why would anyone do that? But they always choose because either it's to make amends or to take it easier. It's always about learning and growing for the soul and the other souls it shares its life with. The soul is trying to get balance and harmony and to remember love and unity. That's the goal.

The soul always has the chance on earth to see things differently: to choose their actions or responses differently— to not react subconsciously, but to respond consciously on a higher level despite what other souls inflict on them in an attempt to balance the score. The more evolved a soul is the more it will work from its conscious responses and not its unconscious reactions.

A person can wake up at anytime during its earth life and end the patterns its carried through many lives.

Aug 13

Your pre-birth blueprint is a blueprint; it is not a detailed step by step, every step of the way manifesto or mandate. It is a guide to what you want to learn and accomplish in that life. Accidents are not always planned but can be from simple unconsciousness from not being in the now moment of what you're doing—just being reckless. Those accidents are usually minor and can be major, and are intended to wake you back to consciousness. Large accidents with a number of people dying are usually part of the pre-birth blueprint. If you've noticed they don't happen all that often in comparison to individual accidents. If you slice your finger —that's an accident due to unconsciousness. Being accident prone is a deeper need for attention, as well as sabotaging yourself. Your broken leg was due to a repetition in thought that wasn't well defined and also not being in the moment consciously. The universe will answer when you affirm or repeat the same words over and over. That's why you need to choose your thoughts that become words carefully. You didn't mean that you wanted to break your leg so you could have a break, but that's what happened.

Was that part of your pre-birth blueprint? Yes and no. Because it was a wake up call for you on your repetitive thoughts and that was part of your blueprint. All accidents can be wake up calls if you'll let them be, and waking up is one of your goals. So however that plays out—kindly or dramatically—is what it's all about. We all get our own attention in whatever way we can to help us reach our goals.

Aug 16

As we said, the ego is just an idea or thought about yourself that you carry around with you on earth to define and defend yourself against others. And because of the fear of death, which is ridiculous when you realize how much you really don't need it and don't have to deal with it here. Without an ego, there's perfect peace and harmony between souls. Only the ego can feel hurt or anger at another person's actions. You need to know that defending yourself and standing up for yourself—in other words having integrity—are not the same thing. Defense comes from insecurity and integrity comes from confidence of knowing who you are, which is never being a doormat. Just think about the difference between defense and confidence and you'll know if you're coming from ego or from your soul. You can change all those "you's" to we, because that's a lesson for all. It's one of the great reasons for being born as a human on earth is to learn this.

Aug 23

The time is quickening for the people of the earth to come up to what they want out of their experience. It will be hard to remain complacent for those who want and need change. A new age really is dawning. There is no longer the calm before the storm, the storm has hit and it's traveling around the world to wash away the walls that have held people back from being who they are.

Okay, so that was Zian, who says things in a different way than me. He's more knowledgeable because he's your main guide, as you know, and has been here longer than me. But I'm doing my work to learn more and more. It's really fascinating and fun and peaceful and joyous and motivating and on and on with all those descriptions that make me feel like my real self. It's amazing how we hide our real selves from ourselves until we wake up and not only see our true selves, but can celebrate who we are and then we can truly see others for who they are. The mirror finally reflects the truth, instead of an image of ourselves we hold in our own, confused minds. It's a goal worth opening to—how you see yourself is how you see others. And how you see others is how you see yourself

Aug 26

Just want to go back to the command to" love thy neighbor as thyself". To make it clearer it should probably be "Love your neighbor as well as love yourself." If you think "as thyself", because most people have not learned how to love themselves, and actually in many cases, hate themselves, and because humans are so good at projecting, they end up hating their neighbor as they hate themselves. When you truly love yourself, you can't help but love others and that's when projecting works well. The persons you project love to from your own inner love then have a choice to accept their own love or reject it—that is not up to you. Your job is just to project the love. It's easy to do that here. Although religions teach this command, they really don't understand what it actually means. Most people think that loving themselves is a selfish act, even when they believe in a God who loves them. The ego tends to turn everything upside down and backwards. And it's the ego that makes you think you are better than and less than and does not want you to see yourselves as equals.

Aug 31

As you can see, the state of the world is in transition and is causing much upheaval. But it will turn out to be a good thing, because people are taking back their power which they spent many years giving away. And it always happens at the times when too few people have too much power. And when the people learn how to take over power without misusing it is always a peaceful time in history. A sense of balance is restored for a time and there is a time of balance for a time. That's humanity and earth life for you—never too stagnant and always with something to learn and growth to achieve—a second of remembering unity.

It's definitely an interesting time in earth history and in US history and a bit reminiscent of the time of the Civil War when the much smaller nation was so divided in their beliefs about how the country should be. The civil war is always being fought somewhere, repeating itself in many places and in many ways—even within neighborhoods and within families—so it's nothing new. Whether micro or macro, it's humans biggest challenge and the less evolved find it easier to war than to unify. Peace for them is dull and uninteresting, because of the lack of drama and ego. There is peace and unity here and unconditional love and it's not dull or uninteresting at all. People don't realize how much can be accomplished when they're at peace. How curious, creative and constructive life can be when we're at peace and when we're unified in that peace.

Peacefully yours, Courtney. Thanks for listening. Love to all.

Sept 7

The tide is turning. History is being repeated, but that is when the lives of people get pushed into the next phase. And the pendulum starts rising up again. It's not an overnight happening, but it is happening. People usually just get caught up and aren't aware of what's going on. They live their lives from the inside of their thoughts instead of as an aware witness to the events. As a witness you can stand outside of it and watch and not be swept up in the events—much like our perspective. It's not an easy thing to do when you're on earth in a body unless you learn to rise above the situation that pulls you into your body and emotions and reactions. Being a witness is as much of an experience as being in the middle of chaos. It's just that the experience comes from a place of calm and peace and non-judgment and knowing you will not be harmed by what's happening in the world. You're seeing it's the level of consciousness you need to get to see things as they really are beyond the five senses you regularly listen to. It's not an easy thing to explain, but many people have reached this state of consciousness at least once in their lives. Everyone can rise above and experience the present moment and the peace that is at the center of them.

When you find yourself in the middle of a tense situation, you only need to breathe deeply to pull yourself out of it and your consciousness will rise, even for that second of your breath. Try it! As many times a day as you need to. A conscious breath reconnects you to your spirit.

Sept 13

As I mentioned before, about our life review we go through when we come to this side, it is not an easy task to go through, but is necessary for our growth and understanding. Even though we're surrounded by loving, non-judgmental energy, it is both an objective and subjective experience all at the same time. It is much like watching a movie that you can analyze objectively, but you can also feel all the emotions of yourself and the other actors, or people, that you came in contact with during your life. You can see what you did and why you did it; the choices you made without even knowing you had made them; the unconsciousness of your life as well as the times of pure consciousness. This is what helps you decide what to work on while you're here. What you learn here will help with your birth plan for your next life.

It's like getting an idea to build a car and designing it, then building it, and then there's a point where it looks good and it's time to take it on a test drive—be born— to see if it will run as you imagined; if it will be able to take the curves and hills and valleys. Your car is your body and you are the driver. When you're done driving that car, you come back over here and see how the ride went.

Sept 17

As I think I mentioned before, when there is what's called a catastrophe on earth and many people die at the same time, there is also a knowledge here, and, of course, there are the guides and welcomers who busily help what you call the departed as they are departing. It's all done with precision and quickly. For those who literally don't know what hit them, there's an element of surprise when they find themselves without a physical body. For those who see it coming, there is some dread and fear and those may need to sleep for a short time before they become aware of where they are, because those are the last emotions they feel on earth and can knock them out for awhile. It will never last forever. They'll eventually wake up to love surrounding them and begin their journey on this side. There's always lots of support for them.

Sept 21

Remember, God's will is always for good, for love and for unity. It is never to take anything, it is only to give steadily all that's good. Human will is often misguided and leads to many mistakes and suffering that is never needed.

When the state of the world is turmoil, you can bet God is not involved. In fact, it is because God is not involved that it is in a state of turmoil. Only ego can cause turmoil. You've heard that ego is an acronym for "edging God out" and that sums it up perfectly. Listening to the ego will never get you to where you need to go. It's like a temporary fix that satisfies you for the moment, but can never sustain itself in the long run. But just like drugs, that temporary fix leads to more and more, getting you nowhere and never bringing joy. And the more you need an ego fix, the more you use relationships to get it and that will never bring love and unity. God's will for us is joy, love and unity. The ego's will is to promote separation, adversity, and dysfunction. You can't get away from the source of who we are, but you can cover up the source by listening to a voice that tells you that we're all separate and therefore you need to defend yourself to preserve yourself. It's so crazy because it's the total opposite of how we could live on earth. Okay, all for now. I love you all.

Sept 28

People fear death because of the "unknown" factor, because they can't see the person anymore and aren't really sure where they went. But, life is an unknown. You never really quite know what today or tomorrow will bring either. You may feel it will be some way or you might plan it to be some way and then something appears and then an unknown happens. These unknowns happen all through life and can change everything you thought you knew. If you're really in touch with your life, which basically is thought of as psychic, you can know something in advance, but most people aren't that attuned. Most people go through their lives surprised by the unknowns that pop up. But most people don't go through life being afraid of the next day and what might happen.

An optimist looks to the next day as an adventure. A pessimist looks at the next day as a possible obstacle to their dreams. But, the unknowns will keep on popping up here and there. You can live with hope or fear—it's a choice. The unknowns will still pop up regardless. And the end of the physical body will happen no matter which you are. Just a choice on how you decide to live your life and experience your passing from that life, whether you know when it will happen or not. And life keeps going on regardless with nothing to fear.

Oct 4

As I've said before, beliefs can lead to unity because of those who agree with your beliefs and also to division from people who don't agree with your beliefs. Since the beliefs aren't truth, they never lead to total unity. They end up being just games you play with one another on earth. You will save yourselves a lot of trouble and misery if you take your beliefs and other's beliefs lightly, knowing they're just temporary. And although they seem to cause real effects, in the end they don't. There are no beliefs here, just gaining knowledge and action toward that knowledge. You do see the truth here and what can be on earth, it's just there is that forgetfulness that comes over most people. The truth does stay with you, inside, even just a little bit, and when you feel it in your heart you never have to defend against anything, because there is a peace you feel that doesn't waver. Truth can't be changed like beliefs can. And truth never divides or starts wars. The truth is within everyone, it's just a matter of opening to it and remembering it and feeling it.

There is this thing about standing up for your truth and that's true to a degree. That's called integrity. That's called being yourself, being comfortable in your own skin. But remember your truth in this life is not necessarily your truth in your next life or the one before this life. When you find your truth in the life you're now living, hopefully it makes you more compassionate as you evolve through lives. But it still comes down to one truth and that is that we all come from one source of unity and love.

Integrity is a feeling of unity within yourself, it's when your inside and outside match. To be truly unified, it needs to include all others. Integrity is a great starting place.

Oct 10

I said: (The Poem you wrote: "Conversations Through the Bathroom Door", that I was wondering where it was for the past 10 months? A friend of mine said she had a poem that Courtney had sent to her and I had no idea about. When she read it to me, I was thrilled, because it was the "Conversations" poem that I couldn't find. She sent it to me and an hour before I received it, I unexpectedly found my copy. I wasn't going to think about making this a book unless I had that poem that she wanted to start her book with.)

As we said, "everything happens in its perfect time". And that was even magnified by two.

Act on it when it feels right to you, but don't doubt that it will get done in its perfect time. No rush.When it feels right, it will feel right and there will be no doubt about it. That's how all things should be done, but that's not always practical on your earth plane. Don't sweat it one way or the other. Do know that when you act from your soul, everything you do is easier and that's something everyone has experienced at least once. So you do know what I'm talking about. Have an easy day. I love you.

October 15

I asked: (What about all the anti-abortion/anti-choice laws sweeping the country?)

They believe—there's that word again—that life begins at conception, even though they don't realize there is never a time that there's not life. Anyway, with that belief it follows that if you end it, you're killing a human life. But that life is just a potential of a human life, just as a carrot seed is the potential of an edible carrot. The biological process of a sperm and egg getting together to grow and make a body that contains a soul that can then experience the physical aspects of earth is awesome, but what soul wants to go from the freedom and expansion of here to a tiny, little containment for a time before it can really experience life on earth? I'll tell you: not most. It's not that the soul isn't getting ready for its birth on earth or that it can't come and go between here and there, but no soul wants to be that confined until it needs to be. Even after birth, the soul continues to come and go while the body grows bigger to not feel so confining. Newborns sleep a lot because they are going back and forth, not because they're so tired. And they remain connected to this side for months and sometimes years. Imaginary friends, anyone?

An embryo and a fetus are on life support through the umbilical cord until the time they have developed enough to live on their own. No human—baby or adult, can live on its own without help from others, but that's another story that is not being considered in this question. Quality of life is not being considered, but there are souls who will still decide to come in despite circumstances. A soul will choose, whether it's this time or another time, but the soul is not in that embryo and will never die.

I was being kept alive on life support through another type of tube to sustain a body that was no longer going to function. When I was taken off, I was able to go on. A fetus is on life support until the time they can have a body that does function independently and go on to live on earth. It's like just the opposite and the same. Whether there's an abortion or not doesn't matter that much to the soul. Nothing is going to kill it.

So the argument will go on, but it doesn't really change the truth. All arguments are based on differing beliefs and beliefs never change the truth. Now, it might sound like I'm saying do whatever you want, because the truth won't change no matter what you do. And, that is actually the truth, but that's not why you're coming and living on earth. The reason you're born to earth is to learn about who we really are and it's not to slaughter, torture, neglect or abuse each other. It's to recognize that we're all related and treat each other with kindness. That's what unifies. That's what love is. Everything else is ego—just an idea that sharing and helping and lifting each other is somehow taking away from us. That if someone has less that they are less and if someone has more that they are more. That's not the truth.

We're all in this together and the sooner people realize this, the happier they'll be. Joy is the gift of knowing and doing this. Remember, none of this is about your body, it's about your soul—the spark that inhabits your body. The body's temporary, as you know, but your soul is forever and it changes and grows. Your spirit is always what it always has been and it knows the truth of who we are.

Oct 18

As I mentioned sometime ago, the people would rise up like in the French Revolution—well, they are, aren't they? *(Occupy Wallstreet all over the country)* Because the people, the average person is the majority and will only be blind for so long until they say "no more". The pendulum cannot stay up forever without swinging.

Oct 25

Good morning. I am still involved in helping to raise the veil between your side and this side to facilitate the light being seen by more and more people. It's an awesome challenge, but it is happening across earth, even though so much of what you see and hear and read sounds so dire. There is also good news when you look for it. But good news doesn't sell as well, mainly because people use the bad news to make their life seem a little better than what they're seeing and reading and hearing about. Also, people have a weird interest in mayhem and horror. And people kind of like the idea that's been taught to them of good vs. evil. Most of history shows this and then it's promoted in movies and books and the news.

Unity sounds rather bland compared, but seeing real unity is uplifting and joyful. That's a reason religion and churches and temples and mosques were formed. Just go to a Black, Baptist church and you'll see and experience joy and unity. The energy is so great that it lifts everyone up to a level that you can feel in your soul. Go to a Unity Church and you'll see and experience unity and peace and joy on a calmer level. Each church, temple or mosque brings a sense of unity for a period of time and attracts souls that resonate with the energy of the place.

Of course, there are still churches that teach the fear of God and try to scare people into being good and righteous, but the message is off and doesn't promote joy. They are all trying to understand God and although it might take awhile, when they come to this side, they'll learn there is no room for fear of God or anything.

The division the world is experiencing is not so much good vs. evil, but old vs. new; past vs. future, even though the present moment is the only moment you can actually live. The vibration on earth is rising and that creates some chaos for awhile. Nothing to worry about. Just focus on the light peeking through. Love to all.

Nov 2

Just want to clarify, since you asked: Kindness isn't the same thing as being polite or being nice. Kindness can sometimes look harsh. Stopping enabling someone can be the kindest thing you can do. Kicking someone out of your life who is being a real negative influence can be a kindness, not only to yourself, but to that other person. The other person may not think of it that way until they awaken, but they will get it someday. So, don't confuse kindness with being nice.

Nov 4

The life beyond is so fascinating and really never to be feared if you live your life with kindness a little more each day. Humans make mistakes, for sure, but they don't have to keep making them. That's the lesson to learn. You'll make mistakes, learn from them and move on. Others will harm you and as you forgive them for their mistakes you can move on. The rewards will not only be great while you're on earth, but greater still over here. Even when you didn't learn from your mistakes, you always have another opportunity here. Those people who others see as dark souls are people who have been abused to the point that they feel they can't forgive and take that hurt into themselves so deeply that they become the hurt and can't do anything but hurt themselves and others. No one can hurt another unless they've been hurt. They don't learn from their mistakes while they are in bodies unless someone can get through to them while they're still there. They do have a harder time adjusting and accepting the love that surrounds them over here. Just as their earth life is hell, so does this sometimes feel like hell because they take hell with them.

It is not an eternal hell, though. Everyone will eventually awaken. It can't be any other way because all souls will eventually recognize their spirit as who they actually are. Our spirit is unchanging and is only love and that is eternal.

Nov 9

Every day is a new time to start again. Actually every minute is. You can change your mind at any second. Life is fluid, always changing even if you don't always see it in the physical world. Your thoughts change from one second to the next unless you get caught up in a loop, like a record getting stuck in a groove. This especially is a problem if the stuck thoughts are negative. If you've ever had the experience of losing your breath or of almost drowning, you know you have to use your awareness and your will to consciously breathe again. It's the same with a loop of negative thoughts; you have to first become aware and then consciously bring positive thoughts to your mind, otherwise you will drown in despair. Just a little hope can change everything. You can get there through prayer or affirmations, just don't try to get there through drugs—it doesn't work. My life was an excellent example of that—trying to change my thoughts and consciousness through something external. Of course, drugs aren't the only thing people use to try to do this. There's food and gambling; there's sex and shopping, the list goes on and on and they all affect not only your life, but those around you to a greater or lesser extent.

The addiction to power and money is playing a big part of consciousness right now and people are becoming more aware of it every day. Awareness is the first step to change. Life on earth is a reflection of what your soul needs.

$\mathcal{N}ov$ 16

Yes, we can see you and hear you, but not in an intrusive way. We check in with you and especially we are drawn to you when you have a lot of thoughts about us—especially good thoughts!

We'll talk about time another time—ha—but did want to talk about forgiveness. The hardest person to forgive is always yourself . Even when what we think of the most awful thing done to us, it is still easier to forgive another than it is to forgive ourselves and without that we will never experience freedom or peace. It's hard to go through a life on earth with no regrets, but on earth, we certainly don't know everything and we make mistakes and the idea is to learn from them. If you can learn from your mistakes, then regrets won't end up being such a big problem because then it will be easier to forgive yourself. Many people feel shame when they make mistakes and also feel shame when another person harms them and it is long lasting until they learn to forgive themselves. It might seems strange, but the most important person to forgive is yourself because without that you can't love yourself and without that you really can't love others. Forgiving yourself is not selfish; it's loving—it is a great gift to yourself and others.

In religion, we look to others to forgive our transgressions, but it doesn't matter how many people forgive us if we don't forgive ourselves. The one thing we need to forgive ourselves for is not being perfect in an imperfect world.

("Like, Maya Angelou says: When you know better, you do better?")

Exactly. But some might say that's not always the case—that even when people know better, they still do awful stuff, but they'll never do it unconsciously again. It will be a choice until they learn forgiveness and mercy for themselves and others.

Nov 18

When you go through your life review here, even though you're surrounded by love and non-judgment, you do see in graphic detail all that was done to you and all the good you did and the mistakes you made and why you did what you did and how it affected others. You see that you were a part of all of it and that forgiving yourself for any mistakes is essential to going on and growing. The energies around you help you do this and those loving energies are around you on earth to help you do the same.

You can do your own life review and forgive yourself even before you do it here. It's a good idea to do, especially if you realize that God's love never changes for you no matter how much you've messed up. You continually loved and forgave me and if you could do that imagine how even greater God's love is. I have forgiven myself for my total ignorance of what I did in that life. We can always start new and that's what time there is for, but it is harder there than here, and here is easier when we do more work there.

Nov 19

Being gay is as temporary as being straight, as being male or female or White, Black, Asian, etc, as being rich or poor or anything associated with being in a physical body. It lasts for the life of your body to experience all different ways of living as a human being and learning what you can for the growth of your soul. Your soul is none of these descriptions and unfortunately, the physical world judges by physical, material, temporary things. These are all to learn compassion, empathy and non-judgment. In some lives you experience the hardships of being different from the norm and it is all meant to serve the growth of your soul by teaching self-love, confidence and integrity. Just as in some lives you experience being part of the norm and are called to show compassion, empathy and non-judgment toward those who aren't part of the norm. There is no physical life on earth that isn't for learning and understanding the illusion of physical life compared to the greater true life. The only thing that is lasting from a physical life is the lessons learned, otherwise it's all temporary and all temporary things are a form of illusion and not reality.

The refrain you hear so often in the Western world is that you only live once or you only have one life to live. And, that's true with the body you are living in now or in my case, just lived, but it's not true that you only have one life to live— you have many lives, in many different bodies—physical and non-physical. How does anyone really think that you're going to learn all you need to know in one physical life, in one physical body? It doesn't even make sense, if you think about how much you can screw up in one life and how short one physical life can be. People need to really think about that. Acknowledging that is not a get-off-free card; in fact, it should make people want to do better and better and learn more and more about love, compassion and unity. That's why you're there. If you don't learn, you will always have the opportunity to learn, because God is mercy and love. Love and mercy do not punish eternally. Love and mercy don't punish at all.

Nov 25

Gratitude is appropriate to talk about at this time. People are thankful for all kinds of things at different times in their lives. There were very few things I was grateful for: you guys when I thought about you, but I saved a lot of my gratitude to getting a fix. I even had a hierarchy of gratitude for my drugs: heroin I was most grateful for, then coke, then the anxiety drugs. I would be grateful when I had a place to live, but then I would take that for granted. I took a lot of things for granted and forgot to be grateful. Sometimes I wouldn't even be grateful for the fix. Remember to be grateful for what you have and what you will have; for being on earth to experience and learn what you went there for, and especially, for the people you touch.

Nov 29

Time is the ultimate paradox. Your time fluctuates, sometimes fast, sometimes slow. Our time stands still. Every moment here is fleeting, but also—this is hard to describe, as paradoxes are always hard to describe—but our time is fleeting and it also contains the element of eternity. It's like each moment here is a life fully lived at a rapid speed.

You're getting pictures in your mind of what I'm saying, but you're having a hard time grasping the words for the pictures. We'll just have to try this again another time.

Dec 22

Another soul has entered the earth plane to learn and grow more, showing extreme courage. Every soul that enters your plane has courage because it's not an easy thing to leave this plane and go back to a confining body knowing what may lie ahead. It is, however, an adventure that isn't easy to pass up when the opportunity presents itself. And, now, the people who have welcomed this soul have the opportunity to love unconditionally and learn and grow themselves. Earth life is all about a soul's relationship to other souls with the added burden, or opportunity, of a physical body which also manifests an ego. Each go around is exciting and daunting, because you have a good idea of what you'll be facing and why you are there. Of course, then you forget most of it.

(My 5ᵗʰ grandchild, and second granddaughter, was born the night before to my youngest daughter, Brecken.)

Dec 28

Good morning and it is. What we do here is through love and determination. Now, being determined can sound willful, but it really means to make up your mind to accomplish a goal. It is the passion and energy behind what's needed to be done. It's very hard to stop anyone who is determined. Our souls are determined to grow and evolve, even when our egos and physical bodies try to counteract that determination.

God has already determined that we are all perfect and belong together and with "him". And so it is. It's just us who have trouble with this concept and have developed a soul and ego who think they have to do something to make it happen. And that is why the soul makes what seems like a journey to get back to where we never have left.

I threw away my life, because I only lived one way and that was to take. That's not exactly true, because I did try to give when I was sane enough and it's what I wanted to do—always. A relationship with drugs becomes all-consuming and then there's nothing left over for others. Obviously, drugs are not the only thing that can become all-consuming and take you away from what's really important—like friends and family.

See, there has to be a balance between giving and taking to lead a stable life. If you only take or you only give, it ends up being almost the same—self-serving. It's easy to see a taker as self-serving, but harder to see an over-giver as the same. But, think about it. Relationships need give and take and if you're only doing one or the other, then you're only in a relationship with yourself without real regard to others who you may be hurting by giving too much or taking too much. Give and take also applies to yourself because it expands you so that you can have relationships with others that benefit all concerned. Self-love and self- centeredness are not the same thing. One is from God and the other from the ego. Guess which is which! Take care of yourself and you can take care of others. Give to yourself and you can give to others. It's the over-doing that keeps you off balance and ultimately regretful. If you learn that lesson while you're there, you won't have to repeat it.

I asked (Didn't Jesus just give?)

No, he didn't. He asked his disciples to follow him and to give up their way of life. He gave them attention, as he asked for their attention. He allowed them to feed him, as he also fed them. They massaged his feet, and he massaged their souls and spirits. Just look at the New Testament, which I know you probably won't do, but it's there. Give and take. Jesus knew his life path and what it would take to show a different way to live. Of course, now we know that through the years, people haven't always listened to the great ones who come to show the way back to where we all began.

Jan 3, 2012 (Bleu's 13th birthday)

Bleu is getting so big and will continue to do well, although he will have his teenage doubts and mental rebellions at times. But, he is growing into a very good human being and you're there to remind him of that— how to be that.

(2012 has been on people's mind because of the Mayan calendar, what's that all about?)

The year is not about endings, but about beginnings. There is always a beginning that follows an ending. It is not to be feared, but looked forward to. It's also to learn to live one day at a time—in the moment—and it will be easier to start doing that for many people, which is really the best way to live. As you can see, people are awakening all over the world. People know that freedom to be yourself is what life should be; not being slaves to others or even their own beliefs that hold them back. That's what the protests are really about— being free and living in a sense of unity and equality. What is ending is the tolerance of being under someone else's thumb. Autocracy has peaked, but the results will take awhile to see.

Give my baby boy a hug for me and let him know my love for him will never die. I love you.

Jan 6

There is no time like the present to be in the present, so when you wander into the past in your mind, you are not re-living the past, you are only remembering things from a distant perception. That isn't necessarily how you saw things at the time and that's how you can change the past to make it more or less positive, which can then change your present. It's said that you can't change the past, but you can change how you view it. That's how forgiveness works.

The future is like looking at a mirage. Until you get there you're never quite sure what you're seeing or if it's real. So forgiving the past and living in the present takes you to the future present which helps you understand that all time is now. Something to contemplate. Now is the only time you can really live and deal with what's in front of you.

(I don't usually remember what was written until I read it later, but the word present kept coming back to me this day. And although there's nothing really new here, I went through my day being more present than usual, because it was a good reminder)

Jan 10

Although greed is the word and it's being shown at a high level throughout the world, it is on stage in the U.S. and people are watching and deciding what that means to not only them but to others. Compassion and empathy are not in the minds of people who want only power.

The pendulum is hitting its high point and then it will begin to swing back into its more neutral state before it can rise again to its positive state of well-being for more people. The neutral state is the time of real assessment and change which propels the rise of the pendulum.

The veil is lifting to let a little more light into the world. Earth is a hard playground and people fall and scrape their knees on the hard surface, but humanity knows how to pick themselves up, bandage their knees and get back on the swings, because there is always a flicker of hope that drives them on to conquer their fears and grow and learn. That's because the soul is always driven to improve and become more of who it is, which is the spirit of good or God—however you define God.

Jan 14

Worry is a choice as are guilt, suspicion, anger, fear, happiness, empathy and on and on. Some of these things don't seem like choices at all, because they seem so automatic and appropriate for whatever circumstances you find yourself in. But, as you recognized yesterday, they are a choice and you can cancel them at will and bring yourself back to the present moment, where they will disappear. It's a neat trick to know to stay in the present.

I'm not doing these writings to answer all of your questions for you, but to help you find the answers yourself.

Jan 24

Good morning. This is the time to talk about what it is to be human and it's not easy because so many things seem to be hidden from your understanding. Not you, but, you know—humans. Understanding the lessons to that understanding is set up by you before you're born. Sometimes even remembering this is set up or not remembering. For most, the discovery is part of the lessons, for if you were to remember it all it could be boring. Discovering why you came leads you to who you are and vice versa.

When you're going down the path of humanity there are road blocks to help you discover your lessons and there are also the answers to how to get through or around or over these blocks if you take the time to see what the block is there to teach you. Try to remember that you are really the one who created it for your own benefit.

What happens so often is that people blame others for the blocks and have a harder time overcoming and learning the lessons. But if you sit quietly and ask what this is for and what you need to learn, with no blame on others or yourself, the answers and direction will come through, because it's already inside of you and was before you even got there. If you're determined to know the answers and learn the lesson you set up, it will come. Not barreling through the blocks, but by listening to your own wisdom and knowledge.

Jan 27

In a way, you're living parallel lives on earth. As I've said, you start out with a birth plan or blueprint of what your life will look like, but the choices you make take you down roads that are the result of that choice. The road you didn't choose is still a road and your spirit knows what it would lead to and on some level your soul is experiencing that road also. Although, I chose to experience the dark side of things and come out of it—you, know, get straight and sober—I pushed it too far and kept choosing the, to me, easy path. Not that I didn't have to work hard at surviving and finding drugs, but it seemed easier than going through withdrawals and trying to be a constructive force in society. That was the road I didn't take, except in my mind. This is so hard to make understandable. That road, that life, I didn't manifest on earth, was still a life that went on without my consciousness and focus, because thoughts are things and are an energy that goes out in the universe. What you call your life is a consequence of your focus. One minute you're conscious of where you are and that you seem to be alive on earth and a split second later your mind wanders to another place. The fact is that you are going back and forth from there to here and to different lives you don't put your focus on and, therefore, don't experience as another life. All time is now and so are all your lives. You will understand this when you're able.

Jan 31

One thing you can't do is live someone else's life for them. You can guide, cajole, witness, listen and pray, but each person has to live their own life for good or bad, in the judgment of other people and themselves. The only one who can judge the entirety of a life is ourselves. We see that clearly when we do our life review here.

God does not judge, the angels don't judge, our guides don't judge. We are the only real judges of our lives in a life review. The judging is done through compassionate perspective.

Feb 3

There are many different realities. People in a physical body tend to think of life in a body on earth is the only reality, but reality is just where you happen to find yourself, whether with or without a physical body.

People who are said to live in a fantasy world are judged as unrealistic or insane, but fantasy is just imagination, sometimes gone awry and then it can be called a mental illness. Reality is also imagination, but usually not as lofty. Like most things on earth, fantasy can be constructive or destructive: Yin/Yang, duality, and all of that.

Reality is as just as much of a myth as is fantasy. On earth, people agree on what is real and what is not. That's called a norm in social science. Everyone has a consensus on some of that reality, such as seasons, time, etc. even though, everyone has their own reality. When I had a body on earth, my reality was much different than yours.

Since you wanted to know a little bit about schizophrenia, I'll give you a little bit of information. Schizophrenia is a little like autism in that it is living in two worlds at once. Schizophrenics are, unfortunately, in touch with the lower planes where they are subject to the souls who perceive themselves in a hell-like place that I mentioned before. It is not like multiple personality or possession. These souls gather around the person, but do not take them over completely. They talk to them, they yell at them, they suggest to them and are always trying to get their attention. These souls try to live vicariously through the person and make them do things that the souls want to do. They are like swarms of mosquitoes constantly buzzing around your head until the person can barely hear anything else but these voices. Being a drug addict is bad enough, but being a schizophrenic would be a hard life lesson. No one is doomed forever; neither the souls on the lower planes or the afflicted.

Personally, I'm grateful I didn't end up on one of those lower planes, but hell was not something you taught or I believed or expected. Even though I lived a hellish life on earth as so many people do.

Feb 10

Your perception of things is what makes your reality. Everyone's perceptions are filtered through their experiences and uniqueness, so that everyone's reality is their own. That is why there can never be one true reality in the physical world. There can't be a complete consensus, but there can be tolerance and even agreement on other's realities.

There is only one true reality and that is God's—that sees and knows the truth of who we are beyond perceptions and beliefs. We're all part of that God or home that we're destined to return to, but have never, in reality, ever left. It appears to be a process, but only for your body, mind and soul. Our spirit is always home.

(I felt there was much more she wanted to say about this that I just couldn't receive at this time. Hopefully, she'll talk more about it another time and I'll be evolved enough to get it).

Feb 18

(Happy Birthday, Courtney. This would have been your 42nd)

Sorry, I couldn't be with you physically, but I was there as you remembered and I felt the love you sent to me. We always feel the love when you send it and it helps our growth and helps our soul. It's like a warm, sparkly glow that encompasses us. I know that when you feel us, it's more like a full body chill that touches your soul. That's because our energy changes the atmosphere around you.

There is still so much to do and say, but for now, I'll just say thank you and I love you. Love to all.

My Thanks

To my husband, Richard, for his love and encouragement. To my daughters, Courtney, Sherstin and Brecken and their wonderful kids, my grandchildren: Malik, Bleu, Devin, Tayten and Layla. And to the one who is yet to come. I love you all.

To my friends, Nancy Doonan, Mary Pat Harrington and Carol Nelson who have been with me through this life and many lives before. I love you.